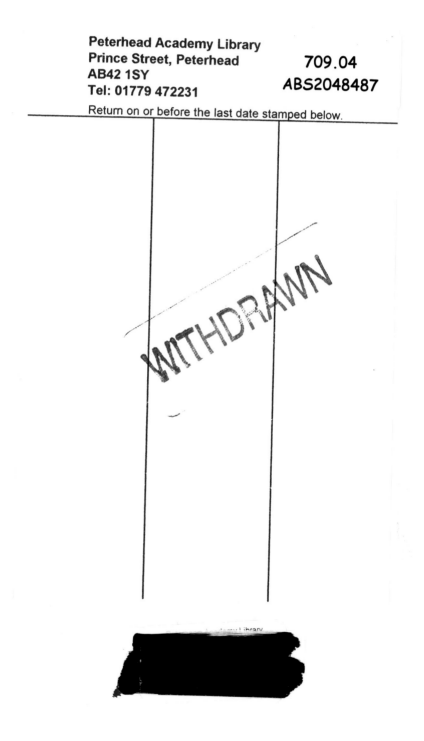

20TH CENTURY ART

1940-60

ART *in* emotion

A HISTORY OF MODERN ART

20TH CENTURY ART – 1940–60
was produced by

David West 🕴 Children's Books
7 Princeton Court
55 Felsham Road
London SW15 1AZ

Picture Research: Brooks Krikler Research
Picture Editor: Carlotta Cooper

First published in Great Britain in 2000 by
Heinemann Library, Halley Court, Jordan Hill,
Oxford OX2 8EJ, a division of Reed Educational and
Professional Publishing Limited.

OXFORD MELBOURNE AUCKLAND
JOHANNESBURG BLANTYRE GABORONE
IBADAN PORTSMOUTH (NH) USA CHICAGO

04 03 02 01 00
10 9 8 7 6 5 4 3 2 1

ISBN 0 431 11603 2 (HB)
ISBN 0 431 11610 5 (PB)

British Library Cataloguing in Publication Data

Gaff, Jackie
1940–1960 art in emotion. -
(Twentieth century art)
1. Art, Modern - 20th century - Juvenile literature
I. Title
709'.044

Printed and bound in Italy

PHOTO CREDITS :
Abbreviations: t-top, m-middle, b-bottom, r-right, l-
left, c-centre.

Front cover & page 17 - AKG London@Kate Rothko
& Christopher Rothko / DACS 2000. Pages 3, 4-5, 6
both, 10r, 14 both, 15b, 22t, 23l & 26b AKG London.
4, 8 both, 9b, 10l, 12 both, 12-13, 16 both, 19r, 20t,
21b, 24, 25b, 26t, 27b & 28 both - Corbis. 5 - Tate
Gallery©Eduardo Paolozzi 2000. All rights reserved,
DACS. 7 & 13 - Tate Gallery©ADAGP, Paris &
DACS, London 2000. 9 - Tate Gallery. 11 - Bridgeman
Art Library©ARS, New York & DACS, London 2000.
11b & 18r - Tate Gallery Archive. 15t - Bridgeman
Art Library©William de Kooning Revocable Trust /
ARS, New York & DACS, London 2000. 18l -
Bridgeman Art Library. 19l - Bridgeman Art
Library©Estate of David Smith / VAGA, New York /
DACS, London 2000. 20 & 23r - Bridgeman Art
Library©ADAGP, Paris & DACS, London 2000. 21 -
Bridgeman Art Library©DACS 2000. 22b - Private
Collection / Bridgeman Art Library. 25t - Bridgeman
Art Library©Jasper Johns / VAGA, New York / DACS,
London 2000. 27t - Moderna Museet©Untitled Press,
Inc / VAGA, New York / DACS, London 2000. 29 -
Bridgeman Art Library©Richard Hamilton 2000.
All rights reserved, DACS. The publishers acknowledge
that the colour of the Cover image and page 17 is
inaccurate. It will be corrected in future editions of the
book.

*The dates in brackets after a person's name
give the years that he or she lived.
The date that follows a painting's title and the
artist's name, gives the year it was painted.
'C.' stands for circa, meaning about or
approximately.*

*An explanation of difficult words can be
found in the glossary on page 30.*

20TH CENTURY ART

1940-60

ART *in* emotion

A HISTORY OF MODERN ART

Jackie Gaff

Heinemann
LIBRARY

CONTENTS

DECADES OF DESPAIR
World War II was brought to an abrupt and brutal end by the dropping of the atomic bombs on the Japanese cities of Hiroshima and Nagasaki in August 1945. As many as 100,000 Japanese civilians were killed by the explosions, and many more died from radiation sickness afterwards. Worldwide, around 15 million soldiers and 50 million civilians were killed during World War II. The deaths continued in the following decades, as the USA and USSR assisted rival sides in wars in Korea, Vietnam, the Middle East and Africa.

TIME OF TENSION

When the 1940s dawned the world was at war. Even after World War II ended in '45, the peace was fragile, with the USA and the USSR building up vast nuclear arsenals and establishing worldwide military and economic alliances. Although neither fought the other directly, a state of hostile tension known as the Cold War existed between the two superpowers for the next 40 years.

In the shadow of the Holocaust and the atomic bomb, the predominant mood of the '40s was disillusion – a loss of faith in everything from systems of government to the methods and purposes of creativity. Few artists turned outwards to society as they had done in the aftermath of World War I, either to criticize it or to contribute ideas for change. Instead many turned inwards, to tap their deepest thoughts and feelings for new ways of expressing their beliefs about the meaning of art and life.

I WAS A RICH MAN'S PLAYTHING, *Eduardo Paolozzi, 1947*
Although they didn't explode on to the art scene until the mid-to-late '50s, Pop Art pictures like this one marked yet another swing of the pendulum of art history – away from the artist's inner world, and back towards social comment and celebration.

NEW WORLD
The American economy was fuelled by World War II and the country was launched on the greatest growth period in its history. The post-war years also saw New York beginning to replace Paris as the capital of world art.

ALBERTO GIACOMETTI

For some of his contemporaries, the skeletally thin figures sculpted by the Swiss artist Alberto Giacometti (1901–66) evoked the starved victims of wartime concentration camps and symbolized the horror and suffering of World War II. For others, the loneliness and fragility of the figures, and the way they seem about to fade away into nothingness, were an expression of existentialist ideas about the nature of human existence.

MAN POINTING
ALBERTO GIACOMETTI, 1947

This delicate sculpture was among the earliest of the tall, emaciated figures for which Giacometti was to become famous. At 1.78 metres high, it was also one of his larger pieces, and quite the opposite of his output during the war years, when his experience of sculpting had been disturbing and bizarre. 'Wanting to create from memory what I have seen,' he wrote about this period, 'to my terror the sculptures became smaller and smaller. They had a likeness only when they were small, yet their dimensions revolted me, and tirelessly I began again, only to end several months later at the same point.' All Giacometti's work from the early '40s was only about 10 centimetres high – not much bigger than a finger!

THREE WALKING MEN, 1948
Even when Giacometti (left) sculpted groups, the individual figures seemed oblivious to one another – reinforcing the sense of loneliness and alienation that many people saw in his work.

BEING AND NOTHINGNESS

One of the most influential thinkers of the post-war period was the French existentialist philosopher Jean-Paul Sartre (1905–80). Existentialism dates back to the 19th century, and is concerned with the nature of existence, or being. Sartre was an atheist, who believed that humans are born into a kind of emptiness, or void, with a future whose only certainty is death. Life is meaningless, unless the individual shapes their future by exerting his or her freedom to choose and takes responsibility for his or her own actions. This emphasis on individuality underlaid much of the focus on self-expression and freedom of action in post-war art.

It was Sartre (left) who was largely responsible for promoting the idea of Giacometti's post-war art being existential – something that the sculptor himself denied.

STRUGGLING TO CREATE

Giacometti himself was more worried about what he was trying to do than with what other people thought about his work. And what he was trying to do was to recreate exactly what he saw – 'I know that it is utterly impossible for me to model, paint or draw a head, for instance, as I see it and yet this is the only thing I am attempting to do…' he said. 'I do not know whether I work in order to make something, or in order to know why I cannot make what I would like to make.' Giacometti was never satisfied with his work, and was constantly destroying it and starting all over again.

SCULPTING THE FIGURE

Giacometti was one of a number of artists who concentrated on representational, or figurative, work during the '40s and '50s. Other leading sculptors to work in this style included American Leonard Baskin (*b.* 1922), Britons Reg Butler (1913–81), Elisabeth Frink (1930–93) and Henry Moore (1898–1986), Frenchwoman Germaine Richier (1904–59), and the Italians Marino Marini (1901–80) and Giacomo Manzù (1908–91).

FRANCIS BACON

Another artist whose work seemed to many to express the post-war mood of gloom and doom was the great Irish-born painter Francis Bacon (1909–92). When his *Three Studies for Figures at the Base of a Crucifixion* were first exhibited in London in 1945, they caused a sensation and turned Bacon overnight into the most talked-about artist in Britain.

POUND OF FLESH

Bacon's subjects were nearly always the human face and body, and his treatment of them was relentlessly gruesome. People were mutilated and distorted into unnatural positions, as though they had been twisted on a torturer's rack. Usually the person was alone, and often imprisoned within metal bars or glass cages. Heads screamed in soundless, unheard agony. Skin and flesh dissolved and dripped from boneless forms.

Backgrounds were often red or black, the colours of blood and death.

MEATY SUBJECT MATTER

Central to Bacon's vision was his sense of the cruelty of life. 'When you go into a butcher's shop,' he said, 'and see how beautiful meat can be and then you think about it, you can think of the whole horror of life – of one thing living off another.'

FIGURE PAINTERS
Other leading representational painters of the post-war period included Britons Graham Sutherland (1903–80, shown left with his 1954 portrait of Winston Churchill) and Lucian Freud (b. 1922), American Larry Rivers (b. 1923), Australian Arthur Boyd (b. 1920) and Frenchman Balthus (b. 1908).

A number of leading artists were employed as official war artists during World War II, including Graham Sutherland (see below). The photograph also became increasingly important, through the efforts of people such as American Lee Miller (1907–77), whose images of Nazi concentration camps helped to convey the horror of the Holocaust.

Miller studied painting in Paris but when this photograph was taken in the early '30s, she was gaining fame as a photographer.

THREE STUDIES FOR FIGURES AT THE BASE OF A CRUCIFIXION
FRANCIS BACON, 1944 (*righthand panel*)

In each of the three panels that make up this nightmarish vision, a subhuman monster writhes in torment, trapped in a boxlike room. Here, in the righthand panel, a head has mutated into a vast, screaming mouth. Bacon was an atheist and, for him, the crucifixion was an expression of human savagery. He said that the panels were sketches for the three Furies – the terrible goddesses of vengeance in ancient Greek and Roman mythology.

Bacon, photographed in '80.

THE SHOCKING TRUTH

Bacon's aim was not simply to shock the people who looked at his paintings, but to alter too their sense of the world – to create something that echoed within their deepest selves and disturbed 'the whole life cycle within a person'. This was quite the opposite to what he described as most art: 'your eye just flows over. It may be charming or nice, but it doesn't change you.'

JACKSON POLLOCK

Despite the continuing significance of individual Europeans such as Bacon and Giacometti, the major new art movement of the post-war years emerged in the USA – where the prime mover was the American painter Jackson Pollock (1912–56).

PAINTING IN ACTION

In '47, Pollock began experimenting with a radically different way of painting. He took his canvas down off his easel and laid it on the floor. Then, instead of brushing on paint, he dripped, flicked and poured it on, using sticks, trowels, knives and even turkey basters. Moving around and sometimes right over the canvas, Pollock worked with his whole body, submerging himself in the act of creation until his paintings swam up from his unconscious to express the deepest levels of his being.

FREE COMPOSITION
Pollock thought that jazz was 'the only other really creative thing' happening in the USA, and his paintings were as improvizational as the bebop jazz of musicians such as Charlie Parker (above).

PLUMBING THE DEPTHS

In the search for a more personal form of expression, Pollock and many other artists were influenced by the theories of the Swiss psychiatrist Carl Jung (1875–1961). Jung expanded earlier ideas about the personal unconscious to include another, universally shared, or collective unconscious. Each individual human, Jung believed, is born with memories of a shared, ancestral history. He called these race memories 'archetypes', and believed that they were revealed through myths and symbols.

Jung held the arts to be an important way of keeping the myths and symbols of the collective unconscious alive.

THE ART OF EMOTION

Pollock was one of a number of American artists who were exploring ways of using paint freely and spontaneously, in order to express powerful thoughts and feelings. Because much of their work was abstract as well as expressive, the movement came to be known as Abstract Expressionism. Pollock was not the sole inventor either of the drip-and-splash technique or of the art movement, but as another leading Abstract Expressionist Willem de Kooning (1904–97) said, he 'broke the ice'.

10

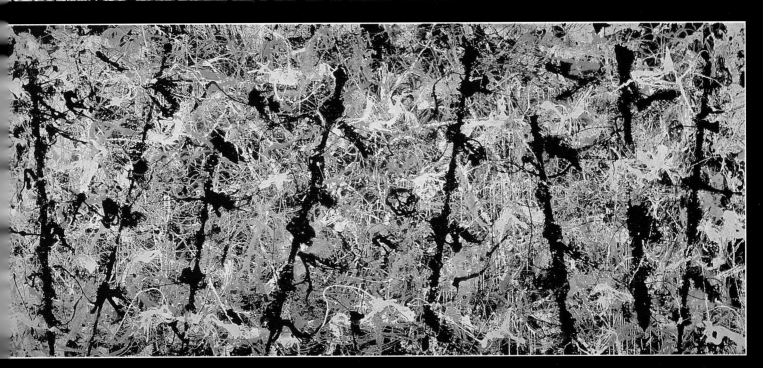

BLUE POLES, NUMBER II
JACKSON POLLOCK, 1952

Instead of painting just with his arm, Pollock used his whole body, dancing around the canvas and splattering it with huge sweeping gestures. He meant the rhythmic swirls of his huge, splattered and splashed canvases to be experienced, not analyzed. Viewers 'should not look *for*,' Pollock explained, 'but look passively – and try to receive what the painting has to offer.'

Pollock may have lost himself in the creative act for much of the time, and his application of paint may look hit and miss, but he did not leave his art to chance. 'When I am painting I have a general notion as to what I am about,' he said. 'I can control the flow of paint; there is no accident.' *Blue Poles* was one of Pollock's last great works – he died in '56, killed when his car crashed.

Jackson Pollock (above left), photographed with friends in New York, in about 1944.

BORN IN THE USA

Abstract Expressionism was the first distinctively new art movement to emerge in the USA and have an international impact. Like all newborns, though, it had parents, and one of the chief influences on Abstract Expressionism was Surrealism. This art movement had grown up in Europe during the '20s, as writers and artists explored the unconscious mind and the world of dreams.

CITY OF SAFETY
The New York skyline was a welcome sight to the lucky few who managed to escape the war in Europe.

SHIFTING SANDS

Another influence on Abstract Expressionism was the art of Native North Americans. Pollock's drip-and-splash technique, for example, was partly inspired by the way the Navajo create sand paintings for special ceremonies by dribbling coloured sands through their fingers.

Navajo sand paintings like this one are made freehand, from memory.

DRAWING ON THE UNCONSCIOUS

Several Surrealists fled from Europe to New York during World War II, including the movement's founder, French poet and critic André Breton (1896–1966), the German-born artist Max Ernst (1891–1976) and the Spaniard Salvador Dalí (1904–89). As far as Surrealism went, though, the American avant-garde was less interested in the dream imagery of Dalí than in Ernst's technique of automatism – a kind of doodling, in which he allowed ideas and images to develop freely from his unconscious. But while the Surrealists tended to use automatism only as a springboard for their work, Abstract Expressionists such as Pollock developed it into the spontaneous creation of an entire painting.

LAND OF THE FREE
Ernst (left) was imprisoned in France after the outbreak of World War II, but managed to escape to the USA in '41 – this photograph shows him being interviewed by an immigration official on his arrival in New York.

12

NEW YORK, NEW YORK

Until World War II, Western art had been dominated by European artists. New movements might have been partly inspired by outside influences – the distorted forms of Cubism by African sculpture, for example – but avant-garde art had developed in Europe, mainly in Paris. As the Nazi grip on Europe tightened, however, many leading artists, not just the Surrealists, set sail for the safety of the USA. This exodus combined with the birth of Abstract Expressionism to shift the focus of avant-garde experimentation from Europe to New York, and saw the city beginning to take Paris' place as the international capital of art.

WATERFALL
ARSHILE GORKY, 1943

The American Arshile Gorky (1904–48) is often described as the last of the great Surrealists and the first of the Abstract Expressionists. Born in Armenia, he arrived in the USA in '20, aged 16. During the next two decades he experimented with a number of styles – Cubism, and geometric and then biomorphic abstraction (based on organic as opposed to geometric forms) – before finding his own distinctive style in the '40s. Surrealism inspired his use of dreamy, free-flowing colour and line, and the way he drew upon his childhood memories and his deepest thoughts and desires for images – *Waterfall* appears abstract, yet at the same time evokes a stream plunging through rocks surrounded by trees and greenery. Yet Gorky's work also shows the spontaneity that was soon to be associated with Abstract Expressionism.

ACTION PAINTING

The Abstract Expressionists preferred to call themselves the New York School, and although their paintings were as individual as their personalities, by the '50s art critics had detected two distinct styles.

ARTISTS IN ACTION

In the work of some artists, including Pollock, it was the painter's actions or gestures that dominated. This style is known as Action Painting and, in addition to Pollock, leading American practitioners included Franz Kline (1910–62), Lee Krasner (1908–84), Robert Motherwell (1915–91) and Dutch-born Willem de Kooning (1904–97). Each developed an individual style – Motherwell and Kline, for instance, mainly used black, sweeping it on to white canvases with huge, expressive brushstrokes.

This rather surreal photograph of Peggy Guggenheim was taken in Venice, in '51.

WOMAN OF MEANS

The American art patron and collector Peggy Guggenheim (1898–1979) played a key role in supporting avant-garde art and in furthering the careers of the Abstract Expressionists. She lived in Europe for much of her life, but spent the war years in New York.

AMBIGUITIES OF STYLE

Not all Abstract Expressionists attempted or even wanted to work as directly from the unconscious as Pollock did, and to complicate matters even further, not all of them created abstract works – at least not all the time. Pollock returned to representation towards the end of his life, while de Kooning moved freely between abstraction and representation throughout his life.

CANDLE IN THE WIND
American sex goddess, and superb comic actress, Marilyn Monroe (1926–62) was one of the most popular pin-ups of the '50s. Since her death, she has become one of the most idolized women of all time.

14

MARILYN MONROE
WILLEM DE KOONING, 1954

In the early '50s, de Kooning began a series of paintings in which recognizable images of women were depicted through wildly energetic, slashing brushstrokes. Part modern pin-up, part ancient fertility goddess, the women in the earliest works were ferociously aggressive, with big grinning mouths and thrusting breasts. By '54, when de Kooning painted *Marilyn Monroe*, the images had become softer and more sensual.

Talking about his Woman series in the '60s, de Kooning (below) said: 'I think it had to do with the idea of the idol, the oracle, and above all the hilariousness of it.'

15

COLOUR FIELD PAINTING

Instead of the gestural marks of Action Painting, other Abstract Expressionists flooded their canvases with large expanses of colour. This style became known as Colour Field Painting, and the pioneering American practitioners included Barnett Newman (1905–70), Ad Reinhardt (1913–67), Clyfford Still (1904–80) and Russian-born Mark Rothko (1903–70).

VARIATIONS ON A THEME

These artists created totally abstract paintings, yet as with other Abstract Expressionists, each had an individual style. Newman's canvases, for example, were almost always monochrome (painted in a single colour), apart from one or more vertical stripes, which he called 'zips'. Rothko, on the other hand, painted hazy, rectangular, cloud-like forms, which seemed to hover and pulsate above the rest of the canvas.

SIZE MATTERS

Size was important to all Abstract Expressionists – many of their paintings were bigger than large windows, some were wall-sized, and they were all supposed to be viewed from close up. Only when 'surrounded' in this way could the viewer begin to share in the artist's experience and feel a response of their own.

THE BIG ISSUE
'To paint a small picture is to place yourself outside your experience...' said Rothko. 'However you paint the larger picture, you are in it.' (His painting opposite measures 1.43 x 1.38 metres.)

CASH BENEFITS
One factor in the establishment of New York as the headquarters of avant-garde art was the financial support given to artists by private patrons and public organizations. In '58, for instance, Rothko was asked to paint a series of murals for the restaurant in the city's new Seagram Building. Rothko eventually gave the murals to London's Tate Gallery, however – probably because he felt a busy restaurant wasn't the most spiritual of places in which to experience his art.

New York's Seagram Building soars to a height of 157 metres.

16

WHITE CLOUD OVER PURPLE
Mark Rothko, 1957

Although abstract, Rothko's paintings are not without subject – 'There is no such thing as good painting about nothing,' he asserted. Like other Abstract Expressionists, Rothko believed in the potential of abstract art to express profound personal and universal truths. 'I'm not interested in the relationship of colour or form or anything else,' he said. 'I'm interested only in expressing basic human emotions – tragedy, ecstasy, doom and so on... The people who weep before my pictures are having the same religious experience as I had when I painted them.'

AMERICAN SCULPTURE

The outstanding American sculptor of the post-war period and, many believe, the most important American sculptor of the 20th century, was David Smith (1906–65).

SPONTANEOUS COMBUSTION

Smith was a close friend of de Kooning and other Abstract Expressionist painters, and shared many of their beliefs and interests, particularly in Surrealism. He created his sculptures from welded iron and steel, working quickly and spontaneously – 'I do not work with a conscious and specific conviction about a piece of sculpture…' he explained. 'It should be a celebration, one of surprise, not one rehearsed.'

ARTISTIC INSPIRATION

Smith began working with welded metal in the early '30s, after seeing pictures of welded sculptures by the Spaniards Pablo Picasso (1881–1973) and Julio González (1876–1942), the first modern artists to make them. In his turn, Smith inspired the abstract metal sculptures of one of the leading British artists of the '60s onwards, Anthony Caro (b. 1924).

BOX OF TRICKS

Another influential American sculptor of the period was Joseph Cornell (1903–1972), one of the pioneers of assemblage (art made from found objects). Cornell's sculptures were a magical and very personal interweaving of memory and imagination. He scavenged junk shops and flea markets for objects, later arranging his finds with photographs, maps and his own mementoes into small wooden boxes.

NIGHT SONGS, *Joseph Cornell, c. 1953*

CUBI XIX
DAVID SMITH, 1964

Smith's series of *Cubi* sculptures were his last great achievement – he was killed when his truck crashed in '65. He gained experience in metalworking through jobs in a car factory in the mid-'20s and constructing locomotives during World War II. Like that of most artists, Smith's work went through various stages. In the late '30s, for instance, he began using found objects such as industrial tools, while during the early '40s he experimented with biomorphic abstraction. Sometimes he painted his sculptures in bright colours, others were designed to rust, while the mirror-like stainless steel surfaces of his geometric *Cubi* sculptures reflected natural sunlight and colour.

'Metal itself possesses little art history,' Smith said. 'What associations it possesses are those of this century: power, structure, movement, progress, suspension, brutality.'

18

CREATIVE EXAMPLES

Other leading American sculptors of the period included Isamu Noguchi (1904–88), Alexander Calder (1898–1976), Russian-born Naum Gabo (1890–1977) and Russian-born Louise Nevelson (1899–1988). Noguchi is best known for his stone-carvings of biomorphic abstract forms. Calder and Gabo also made abstract sculptures, and they had both pioneered kinetic art (art that incorporates movement) in the '20s and '30s.

WALL OF FAME
Another pioneer of assemblage, Nevelson began making the wall-sized abstract sculptures for which she became famous in the late '50s. She built them from shallow box shapes, which she filled with wooden found objects (everything from toilet seats to chair legs), finally spraying the entire assemblage with black paint.

JEAN DUBUFFET

Outside the USA, the hunt was also on for more expressive and spontaneous forms of creativity, and one of the most experimental European artists was the Frenchman Jean Dubuffet (1901–85).

LA CALIPETTE
JEAN DUBUFFET, 1961

Flat, simplified people, dogs and cars bustle along a wobbly street, against a backdrop of colourful graffiti – Dubuffet's style was deliberately like that of a young child.

Dubuffet worked for many years as a wine merchant, and he didn't take up art full time until 1942.

20

THE EYES OF A CHILD

Dubuffet tried to reinvent art by looking at the world with fresh eyes, uncluttered by history or tradition. Influenced by the ideas of the Surrealists, he admired the simplicity, spontaneity and directness of art created by the untutored, those outside the established, professional art world – the pictures made by children and the mentally ill, and the art of the street, graffiti. He coined the term Art Brut (French for 'raw or rough art') to describe it, and set up an organization to collect and study it. 'There is only one way to paint well,' Dubuffet said, 'while there are a thousand ways to paint badly: they are what I'm curious about; it's from them that I expect something new, that I hope for revelations.'

CHILD III, *Karel Appel, 1951*
Among those who shared Dubuffet's interest in the art of children was the Dutch artist Karel Appel (b. 1921). 'You have to learn it all,' Appel said, 'then forget it and start again like a child.'

WRITING ON THE WALL

Although graffiti dates back to ancient times – it covered the walls of the Roman city of Pompeii, for example – only in the 20th century have people begun to think of it as art and not simply vandalism. Its high point was the '80s, when its superstars were American graffiti artists Keith Haring (1958–90) and Jean-Michel Basquiat (1960–88).

In '86, Haring opened a shop to sell T-shirts and other goods emblazoned with his artwork.

THE MATERIALS OF THE STREET

Dubuffet experimented with materials as well as with ways of seeing. By '46 he was beginning to copy the texture of the walls on which graffiti is usually found – building a surface up from substances such as plaster and putty, then scratching into it. He remained fascinated by materials throughout his life, making collages from butterfly wings, leaves, flowers and tinfoil, and sculptures from lumps of coal, tree roots, driftwood, painted metal and carved polystyrene.

ART MATTERS

In the post-war years, artists of all nationalities were, like Dubuffet, exploring the expressive qualities both of painting and of the materials, or matter, of art.

PAINT AND PASTE

The French artist Jean Fautrier (1898–1964), for example, built his paintings from layers of a thick mixture of cement, plaster and paint. The roughly formed faces of his *Hostage* series (begun 1943) were inspired by wartime experiences and suggest death, decay and horror. The richly textured paintings of the Spaniard Antoni Tàpies (*b.* 1923) were constructed from found materials such as string, rags and card, and paint thickened with sand, marble dust and other substances.

*FINDERS KEEPERS
Italian Alberto Burri (1915–95) worked with sacking and other found materials.*

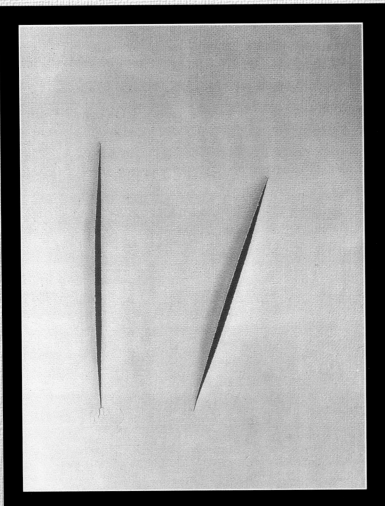

SPATIAL CONCEPT
LUCIO FONTANA, 1959

Argentinian-born Italian Lucio Fontana (1899–1968) launched his Spatialism movement in the late '40s, calling for a new art for a new age. Among other things, he wanted to ditch any remnants of the traditional illusion of space, or perspectival depth, in painting. In '49, he introduced actual space into his work by punching holes into his paintings, and nine years later, he began creating the slashed, monochrome canvases for which he is best known, such as the one shown here. Fontana wanted to fuse colour and form with sound, movement, time and space, and he claimed that 'a new art will be possible only with light and television'. In his spatial environments, he was one of the first artists to use neon lighting to project colour and form into real, three-dimensional space.

SCRIBBLES AND DRIBBLES

Other artists were more concerned with the act of painting than with the materials. Gestural and expressive, their style was similar to American Action Painting – although, in the early years at least, it developed independently of events in the USA. By the mid-'40s, for example, expressive brushstrokes and paint squiggles were being used in a free, spontaneous way by the German-born artist Wols (the pen name of Wolfgang Schulze, 1913–51). Other leading gestural painters included Pierre Soulages (*b.* 1919) and Georges Mathieu (*b.* 1921) of France, German-born Hans Hartung (1904–89) and Canadian-born Jean-Paul Riopelle (*b.* 1923).

ART AT WAR
Like other post-war artists, Tàpies attacked the conventions of fine art through his use of unusual materials.

T57-13E
HANS HARTUNG, 1957

Hartung began painting abstracts in '22, when only 17, and had developed his elegant, gestural style by the late '30s. His work may appear spontaneously expressive, but he believed in planning and forethought, and said that the artist 'must try to preserve in the performance, the freshness, directness and spontaneity characteristic of improvization'. Although born in Germany, Hartung spent most of his life in France, becoming a French citizen in '46. He gave his paintings 'T' numbers, from the French word *toile* meaning 'canvas', in place of titles.

JASPER JOHNS

In the USA, by the mid-1950s, a reaction was setting in towards the soul-searching of Abstract Expressionism, and one of the chief agents of change was the young American artist Jasper Johns (*b.* 1930).

AMERICAN DREAM

In '55, when he was 25, Johns dreamt of painting a large American flag. 'The next morning,' he said, 'I went out and bought the materials to begin it.' The striking thing about Johns' painting, however, was that unlike any Surrealist or Abstract Expressionist dream-inspired work, it did not draw on the world of the unconscious. Apart from its heavily textured surface, Johns' painting was almost an exact copy of the real American flag.

NUMBER CRUNCHING
Johns also made paintings of everyday signs, such as letters of the alphabet, and the numbers you can see on the wall behind him in this photograph.

THREE FLAGS
JASPER JOHNS, 1958

Johns' 1955 painting of the American flag was the first of a series which included this set of three canvases. He also worked on a series of *Target* paintings (with painted rings, like those on a shooting target), and made small sculptures of everyday objects, such as beer cans and light bulbs. For Johns, these 'found images' (ones that are not invented by the artist because they already exist) made his art less personal and more objective. 'Using the design of the American flag took care of a great deal for me because I didn't have to design it,' he explained. 'So I went on to similar things like targets – things the mind already knows.'

FLAUNTING THE FLAG

Johns wanted to move away from the subjectivity (based on personal thoughts and feelings) of avant-garde American art and make something less emotional and more objective – his work was not obviously about himself, the artist, for example, but about an object, the flag. This may sound fairly straightforward, but at the same time, Johns also raised all sorts of complex questions about the meaning of art, the meaning of objects in the real world, and the relationships between them. For Johns had not chosen any old object – he had chosen the symbol of American national and cultural identity.

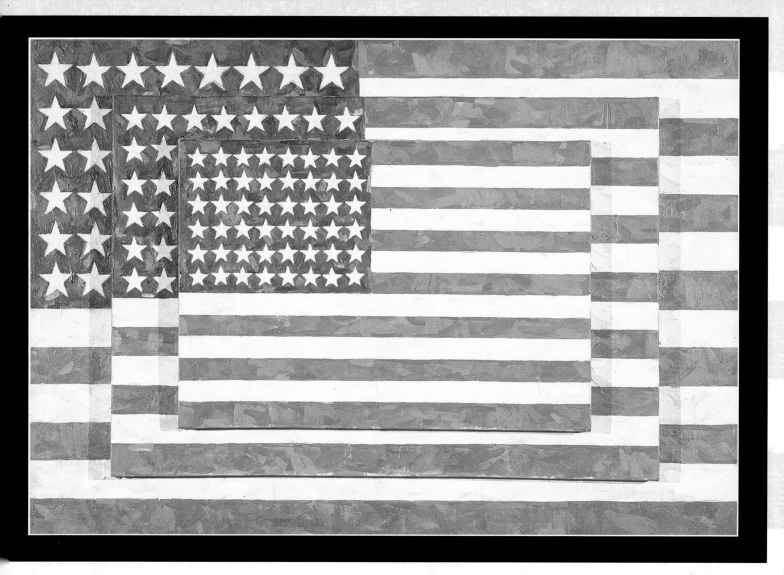

WHEELER DEALER
One of the most influential art dealers of the 20th century, Italian-born American Leo Castelli (b. 1907) launched Johns' career with an exhibition in '58.

OBJECT LESSON

Part of what Johns was doing was highlighting the powerful messages that objects and images can convey. When looking at a painting of the American flag, for instance, the viewer is invited to think about the flag's symbolic meaning. At the same time, Johns turned the flag into a flat, painted pattern, stripping it of the symbolic and emotional baggage that it would have had if, for instance, it was being held by a soldier in battle or an athlete at the Olympics. On top of all this, Johns' work was also both a painting and a flag – he had bridged the gap between representation (art) and object (real world).

ROBERT RAUSCHENBERG

Johns was not alone in his rebellion against Abstract Expressionism. His friend, the American artist Robert Rauschenberg (*b.* 1925), was just as subversive and an equal influence for change.

ROUGH AND READY

If Johns was interested in the found image, his friend was fascinated by the found object. Rauschenberg began to collage found objects into his work in the mid-'50s, often using junk he had picked up on the streets around his New York home. This was not a new technique, and although Rauschenberg called his works 'combines', they were a form of the assemblage practised by sculptors such as Cornell.

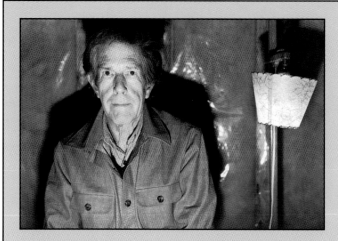

A close friend of Rauschenberg and Johns, Cage (above) greatly influenced their ideas.

MUSICAL GURU

One of the most inspirational figures on the post-war art scene was the American avant-garde composer John Cage (1912–92). Cage was opposed to subjectivity – 'There is no room for emotion in a work of art,' he said – and he valued chance and the everyday. Any sound or noise was music, so in his *4' 33"* ('52), for example, the performer sat silently at the piano while the audience listened to chance sounds in the concert hall or from outside.

CHANCE, NOT CHOICE

However, where Cornell's assemblages were steeped in personal associations, Rauschenberg tried to make his combines impersonal, using whatever came to hand instead of hunting down specific objects. Like Johns, he wanted to abandon the subjectivity of Abstract Expressionism. 'I don't mess around with my subconscious,' he explained. 'I try to keep wide awake. Painting is always strongest when...it appears as a fact, or an inevitability, as opposed to a souvenir or arrangement.'

ARTISTIC GURU
French-born American Marcel Duchamp (1887–1968) was a leading light of the anti-art movement, Dada. As the inventor (in 1913) of the ready-made, he was a huge inspiration to Johns and Rauschenberg.

MONOGRAM
ROBERT RAUSCHENBERG, 1955–59

With its stuffed angora goat and car tyre, *Monogram* was Rauschenberg's most famous combine. Others included *Bed* ('55), made from bedclothes splattered with paint, toothpaste and nail polish, and *Canyon* ('59), which featured a stuffed eagle. Rauschenberg was hugely experimental and soon gave up making combines and moved on to other ideas, including dance and performance art. His *Pelican* ('63), for example, was dedicated to the pioneers of powered flight, the Wright brothers, and took place in a roller-skating rink – Rauschenberg performed on roller-skates, wearing a huge, sail-like parachute.

'Painting relates to both art and life,' said Rauschenberg. 'Neither can be made. (I try to act in that gap between the two.)'

BIRTH OF POP

Pop is short for popular (as in popular culture), and in their use of everyday images and objects, Rauschenberg and Johns were godfathers to the US Pop Art movement of the '60s. Across the Atlantic in Britain, a separate Pop Art movement developed in the '50s.

MESSAGES FOR THE MASSES

British Pop Art grew out of meetings at London's Institute of Contemporary Arts (ICA) from '52 onwards, at which a small group of artists, art critics and architects discussed the imagery and impact of the new age of consumer goods (things bought to satisfy personal needs) and the mass media.

LUXURY LIFESTYLES

European economies were slow to recover in the post-war years, and it wasn't until the mid-'50s that people began to have money in their pockets again for luxuries. The American economy was booming, however, and the ICA group was fascinated by the glossy, colourful lifestyle promoted in the American cinema films, TV programmes, comics, magazines and advertisements that were flooding into Britain.

The Whitechapel Art Gallery opened in London's East End in 1900.

POPULAR PICTURES

In '56, London's Whitechapel Art Gallery was the venue for an exhibition organized by the ICA group on the new popular culture. Called 'This is Tomorrow', it included Hamilton's ground-breaking Pop collage *Just What Is It...?* (opposite).

PIONEERS OF POP

The artistic fathers of British Pop Art were Britons Eduardo Paolozzi (*b.* 1924) and Richard Hamilton (*b.* 1922). It was Hamilton who in '57 came up with a now famous list of the qualities of Pop Art – 'popular, transient, expendable, low-cost, mass-produced, young, witty, sexy, gimmicky, glamorous and big business'!

MASS-MARKETING MEDIUM
Invented in the 1920s, but not widely available until after the war, television was a powerful tool for reaching mass audiences.

28

JUST WHAT IS IT THAT MAKES TODAY'S HOMES SO DIFFERENT, SO APPEALING?

RICHARD HAMILTON, 1956

The answer to Hamilton's question was everything from a new Hoover to a new, muscular body. Was he serious – no, of course not! Hamilton was making a joking, but critical comment about consumerism.

Hamilton made his picture by collaging advertising images, and it was one of the first Pop Art works. It even includes the word 'pop' – on the blown-up lollipop carried by Hamilton's muscle-bound 'hero'.

GLOSSARY

ABSTRACT ART Art that does not attempt to represent the real world, but which instead expresses meaning or emotion through shapes and colours.

ABSTRACT EXPRESSIONISM An art style that emerged in New York during the 1940s, in which artists aimed to express powerful emotions through paint and painting techniques. Also known as the New York School.

ACTION PAINTING A branch of Abstract Expressionism that stressed the expressiveness of the artist's action or gesture.

ART BRUT Art created by those outside the established art world, such as children. The term was coined by Jean Dubuffet in the 1940s.

ASSEMBLAGE The use of found objects to make a work of art. The technique evolved from collage.

BIOMORPHIC ABSTRACTION Abstract art based on organic (rather than geometric) shapes.

COLOUR FIELD PAINTING A branch of Abstract Expressionism that stressed the expressiveness of large expanses of colour.

DADA An anti-sense and anti-tradition movement in art and literature born in Europe and the USA during World War I.

FOUND OBJECT A natural or manufactured object found by an artist and used either in or as a work of art.

HOLOCAUST The mass-extermination by the Nazis of Jews and other races they considered 'undesirable'.

POP ART An art movement that made use of the imagery of consumerism and popular culture. It flourished from the late '50s to the early '70s, mainly in Britain and the USA.

READY-MADE The name given by Marcel Duchamp to manufactured objects he chose at random and presented as works of art.

REPRESENTATIONAL ART Art that portrays things seen in the real world. Also known as figurative art.

SURREALISM A movement in art and literature that grew out of Dada in the '20s. Fascinated by dreams and the unconscious, Surrealists made the real unreal, and the everyday disturbing and strange.

30

TIMELINE

	ART	DESIGN	THEATRE & FILM	BOOKS & MUSIC
0	•*Death of Paul Klee*	•*USA: Raymond Loewy's Lucky Strike design*	•*Chaplin:* The Great Dictator •*First Bugs Bunny cartoon*	•*Ernest Hemingway:* For Whom the Bell Tolls
1	•*Surrealists A. Breton & Ernst arrive in New York*		•*B. Brecht:* Mother Courage •*Orson Welles:* Citizen Kane	•*Dmitri Shostakovich:* Leningrad Symphony
2	•*Edward Hopper:* Nighthawks		•*Ingrid Bergman & H. Bogart star in* Casablanca	•*Irving Berlin's song 'White Christmas'*
3	•*Mondrian:* Broadway Boogie-Woogie	•*Brazil: Oscar Niemeyer's church at Pampulha*	•*Rodgers & Hammerstein's* Oklahoma!	•*Jean-Paul Sartre:* Being and Nothingness
4	•*Bacon:* Three Studies... •*Death of Piet Mondrian*		•*M. Graham & A. Copland:* Appalachian Spring *(ballet)*	•*W. Somerset Maugham:* The Razor's Edge
5	•*Paris: Jean Fautrier's* Hostages *series exhibited*	•*USA: W. Gropius founds The Architects' Collaborative*	•*Roberto Rossellini:* Rome, Open City	•*J. Steinbeck:* Cannery Row •*B. Britten:* Peter Grimes
6	•*Gyula Košice makes first neon-light sculpture*	•*Italy: Vespa scooter designed for Piaggio Co.*	•*Cannes Film Festival first held*	•*William Carlos Williams:* Paterson *(first volume)*
7	•*Jackson Pollock's first Action Paintings*	•*USA: Alvar Aalto's Hall of Residence, MIT (to '49)*	•*Tennessee Williams:* A Streetcar Named Desire	•*Albert Camus:* The Plague •*Anne Frank's Diary*
8	•*Cobra group founded* •*B. Newman:* Onement I		•*Vittorio De Sica:* The Bicycle Thieves	•*Alan Paton:* Cry the Beloved Country
9	•*Fontana first punches holes in his canvases*	•*USA: Philip Johnson's glass home at New Canaan*	•*Arthur Miller:* Death of a Salesman	•*Simone de Beauvoir:* The Second Sex •*G. Orwell:* 1984
0	•*Willem de Kooning:* Excavation & Woman I	•*USA: Mies van der Rohe's Farnsworth House*	•*A. Kurosawa:* Rashomon •*J. Anouilh:* The Rehearsal	•*F. Loesser:* Guys & Dolls •*P. Neruda:* Canto General
1	•*Pablo Picasso:* Massacre in Korea	•*London: Royal Festival Hall (R. Matthews & others)*	•*Alec Guinness stars in* The Lavender Hill Mob *(Crichton)*	•*J.D. Salinger:* The Catcher in the Rye
2	•*Pollock:* Blue Poles, Number II	•*Denmark: Arne Jacobsen's Ant Chair*	•*Gary Cooper stars in Fred Zinnemann's* High Noon	•*John Cage's silent 4' 33"* •*E.B. White:* Charlotte's Web
3	•*Matisse:* The Snail •*L. Rivers:* Washington...	•*USA: Louis I. Kahn's Yale University Art Gallery*	•*S. Beckett:* Waiting for Godot •*A. Miller:* The Crucible	•*Nadine Gordimer:* The Lying Days
4	•*Japan: Yoshihara founds avant-garde Gutai group*	•*France: Le Corbusier's Notre-Dame-du-Haut*	•*Marlon Brando stars in E. Kazan's* On the Waterfront	•*J.R.R. Tolkien:* The Lord of the Rings *(first volume)*
5	•*Johns paints the first of his* Flag *series*	•*W. Germany: Ulm Academy for Design opens*	•*Cary Grant stars in Alfred Hitchcock's* To Catch a Thief	•*Patrick White:* The Tree of Man
6	•*UK Pop Art launched* •*Hamilton:* Just What Is It	•*USA: Eero Saarinen's Tulip Chair*	•*John Osborne:* Look Back in Anger •*Godzilla released*	•*Elvis Presley's first hit, 'Heartbreak Hotel'*
7	•*Deaths of Constantin Brancusi & Diego Rivera*	•*Australia: Jorn Utzon's Sydney Opera House (to '73)*	•*I. Bergman:* The Seventh Seal •*Jean Genet:* The Balcony	•*Jack Kerouac:* On the Road •*L. Bernstein:* West Side Story
8	•*Mark Rothko asked to do Seagram murals*	•*New York: Mies van der Rohe's Seagram Building*	•*Harold Pinter:* The Birthday Party	•*B. Pasternak forced to refuse Nobel Prize for Dr Zhivago*
9	•*Rauschenberg completes* Monogram (from '55)	•*New York: F.L. Wright's Guggenheim Museum*	•*Marilyn Monroe stars in B. Wilder's* Some Like it Hot	•*Death of Buddy Holly* •*Motown label launched*

INDEX

32